GRANDMA'S HOUSE

ISBN: 9798837887505

Published by NspireMe2B Publications
Birmingham, Alabama

Dedication

In loving memory of Tyras J. McKinney

GRANDMA'S
HOUSE

Grandma's house is a place for fun. To swim, hunt, and fish under the sun.

A place our parents won't miss us a piece, especially during the hot summer weeks.

My first favorite thing about grandma's house is, visiting our family and the other grandkids.

With grandpa and aunties and uncles combined, and cousins mistaken for siblings of mine.

My second favorite thing about grandma's house is, there is so much space for all of us kids! Grandma lives on a farm with granddaddy too, let me tell you about the things that there are to do!

There are horses to ride, and cows to feed.

There are goats, but I'm not sure for what reason, beats me.

There are dogs for our protection and hunting too.

There are cats to pet and peacocks to shooooooo!

There are go carts, four wheelers, and trampolines, for jumping high, "Sky's the limit," we sing.

A basketball court hand made by our old man, where we run, jump, and shoot as best as we can.

Lastly, oh lastly, we have a blue pool! Grandma fills it with a hose. Tell me that isn't cool!

Five of us! That's how many it is, yet so much to do on a farm full of kids.

My cousins, I love them like best friends forever, ohh what a feeling when we all get together.

We play inside and out and keep each other busy; our different personalities help keep each other witty.

The oldest is Keke, she loves reading and writing.

Next, there's TJ, he loves action figures and play fighting.

Then, there's Troy, he draws and plays the drums.

Also, you have me, I'm all of them combined in one.

Last but not least, there's An'Ton Ronielle, he's the youngest of us all with curly long hair.

We all love different things, but one thing is the same ... Grandma's house is ours and no one can take that away.

The summer is ending, but I can't let it leave without telling you the best part of Grandma's to me.

It's the love and the memories we will have forever, Thank you grandma and granddaddy for keeping us all together.

To understand the ways of this world is not a giving. In the words of Vencie Lee, "*Just keep on living.*"

"Behind the book with Tessa Shack"

"When I first started this project, it was never my intention to grow it into a book. Initially, I found myself writing through my emotions, which turned into a poem. And once it was no longer a trigger point, the vision for a book arrived." says Tessa.

"At the time, I was deeply mourning the loss of my sibling-cousin and realized the core of our relationship was built at one central location ... our Grandmother's House. Revisiting the best of those intimate memories was a way to honor him and the love generated between us all as a family." she adds.

Tessa made her author's debut with this family friendly short story but she's no stranger to the industry. After earning her degree in Broadcast Journalism at Florida A&M University, she progressed as a freelance writer and currently holds 11 publications.